WOMEN WHO DARE

Women of the Civil War

BY MICHELLE A. KROWL

Pomegranate
SAN FRANCISCO

LIBRARY OF CONGRESS
WASHINGTON, DC

Published by Pomegranate Communications, Inc.
Box 808022, Petaluma CA 94975
800 227 1428; www.pomegranate.com

Pomegranate Europe Ltd.
Unit 1, Heathcote Business Centre, Hurlbutt Road
Warwick, Warwickshire CV34 6TD, UK
[+44] 0 1926 430111; sales@pomeurope.co.uk

Amy Pastan, Series Editor

In association with the Library of Congress, Pomegranate publishes other books in the Women Who Dare®
series, as well as calendars, books of postcards, posters, and Knowledge Cards® featuring daring women.
Please contact the publisher for more information.

Library of Congress Cataloging-in-Publication Data

Krowl, Michelle A.
    Women of the Civil War / by Michelle A. Krowl.
      p. cm. — (Women who dare)
    Includes bibliographical references.
    ISBN 0-7649-3546-1
    1. United States—History—Civil War, 1861–1865—Women. 2. United States—History—Civil War,
1861–1865—Women—Pictorial works. 3. Women—United States—History—19th century. 4. Women—
Confederate States of America—History. 5. Women—United States—History—19th century—Pictorial
works. 6. Women—Confederate States of America—History—Pictorial works. I. Library of Congress. II.
Title. III. Women who dare (Petaluma, Calif.)
    E628.K76 2006
    973.7082—dc22

2005040195

Pomegranate Catalog No. A112
Designed by Harrah Lord, Yellow House Studio, Rockport, ME
Printed in Korea

15 14 13 12 11 10 09 08 07 06   10 9 8 7 6 5 4 3 2 1

FRONT COVER: Clara Barton, "Angel of the Battlefield" LC-USZ62-19319; manuscript poem by Antonia Ford
LC-MSS-45757-7
BACK COVER: Rose Greenhow and daughter at Old Capitol Prison, Washington, DC LC-DIG-CWPBH-04849

PREFACE

FOR TWO HUNDRED YEARS, the Library of Congress, the oldest national cultural institution in the United States, has been gathering materials necessary to tell the stories of women in America. The last third of the twentieth century witnessed a great surge of popular and scholarly interest in women's studies and women's history that has led to an outpouring of works in many formats. Drawing on women's history resources in the collections of the Library of Congress, the Women Who Dare book series is designed to provide readers with an entertaining introduction to the life of a notable American woman or a significant topic in women's history.

From its beginnings in 1800 as a legislative library, the Library of Congress has grown into a national library that houses both a universal collection of knowledge and the mint record of American creativity. Congress' decision to purchase Thomas Jefferson's personal library to replace the books and maps burned during the British occupation in 1814 set the Congressional Library on the path of collecting with the breadth of Jefferson's interests. Not just American imprints were to be acquired, but foreign-language materials as well, and Jefferson's library already included works by American and European women.

The Library of Congress has some 121 million items, largely housed in closed stacks in three buildings on Capitol Hill that contain twenty public reading rooms. The incredible, wide-ranging collections include books, maps, prints, newspapers, broadsides, diaries, letters, posters, musical scores, photographs, audio and video recordings, and documents available only in digital formats. The Library serves first-time users and the most experienced researchers alike.

I hope that you, the reader, will seek and find in the pages of this book information that will further your understanding of women's history. In addition, I hope you will continue to explore the topic of this book in a library near you, in person at the Library of Congress, or by visiting the Library on the World Wide Web at http://www.loc.gov. Happy reading!

—JAMES H. BILLINGTON, The Librarian of Congress

HAIL! GLORIOUS BANNER OF OUR LAND.

GIBSON & CO. LITH. CINCINNATI.

I ask neither pay nor praise, simply a soldier's fare and the sanction of your Excellency to go and do with my might, what ever my hands find to do.
                    —Clara Barton to Governor John A. Andrew of Massachusetts

T he Civil War was the defining event in the lives of many nineteenth-century women, whether they lived in the North or the South. For some, the turmoil of war allowed them to be daring in the name of patriotism. "Daring" came in all shapes and sizes. Some women donned men's clothes and fought as soldiers. Some acted as spies. Some challenged the notion of women's delicate nature by serving as nurses amidst the blood and gore of battlefields and hospitals. Still others offered their voices and their pens on behalf of their country. "It is the story of women who did not urge their brothers and lovers to go to the field," said one source, "without themselves following as far and as closely as the law would let them." Some women did not intend to be left behind.

■ *At the start of the Civil War, women's participation in the conflict was not expected to be much more than allegorical. But over the next four years, women on both sides would do much more.* LC-USZC2-3768

■ *Frances Clayton*

Some female soldiers passed as males thanks to cursory physical examinations, uniforms that were not formfitting, lack of regular personal hygiene by all soldiers, and the likelihood that they stopped menstruating during the physical strain of soldiering. Frances Clayton completed her look by taking on male habits such as smoking, drinking, and swearing. Some women had assumed male identities before the war, usually to secure employment, and were comfortable living as men by the time they joined the army.

BOSTON PUBLIC LIBRARY/RARE BOOKS DEPARTMENT

ALL THE DARING OF A SOLDIER:
WOMEN IN COMBAT

AT LEAST 250 WOMEN are known to have enlisted secretly in the military during the Civil War; certainly many more went undiscovered. The reasons these women joined the army were as varied as the women themselves. Patriotism, desire for adventure, proximity to a particular soldier, and the promise of steady employment or bounty money all proved enticing.

Some women passed themselves off as men to follow husbands or brothers into the field. These women tended to be discovered early in their enlistments, or they left when their men were wounded or if they deserted. Some women maintained their ruses longer, but were eventually found out when wounded in battle. Occasionally a soldier was discovered to be a woman when she gave birth to a baby, which Union General William Rosecrans thought to be "in violation of all military law and of the army regulations."

Other women successfully passed as men throughout the span of their military service. Jennie Hodgers enlisted in the 95th Illinois Infantry as Albert D. J. Cashier, and her regiment saw action in Mississippi and Tennessee. Cashier fought alongside her male comrades, who noticed only that she appeared smaller in stature than the average soldier. A severe bout of diarrhea put her in the hospital in 1863, but she was released before medical authorities discovered her "other" condition. So adept was Hodgers at being a man that she remained Albert Cashier after the war and received a veteran's pension for military service. Only when Cashier was hospitalized in 1911 at the age of approximately sixty-seven was *he* discovered to be a *she*.

Using the alias Lyons Wakeman, Sarah Wakeman joined the 153rd New York State Volunteers, which saw action in the Red River campaign in Louisiana. Like many of her comrades, Wakeman was felled by dysentery rather than a bullet. She died in a New Orleans hospital in 1864 and was buried as Lyons Wakeman, her true identity still undiscovered. It might have remained so had not Lauren Cook Burgess, working in the late twentieth century to promote the role of women in Civil War reenactments, come upon Wakeman's family and gained access to her letters.

Sarah Emma Edmonds enlisted in a Michigan regiment under the name Franklin Thompson. She performed noncombat roles and saw action on Virginia battlefields in 1861–1862. As Thompson, she fell in love with at least two of her comrades, which prompted her to desert in 1863 rather than face exposure and rejection. After reassuming her female identity, Edmonds acted as a nurse and spy for the Union. Interestingly, Edmonds later applied for a veteran's pension based on her military service as Franklin Thompson, explaining that her desertion was the result of an illness she feared would expose her true gender. Bolstered by support from her fellow veterans, Edmonds secured her pension; the desertion charge was overturned.

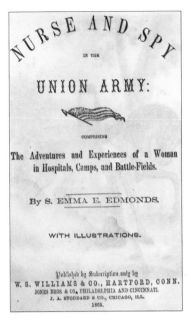

On the Confederate side, Loreta Janeta Velazquez assumed the identity of Harry T. Buford in order to follow her husband into the war, but she headed off to the front alone after his death. She claimed to have participated in several key battles (at times taking temporary command of leaderless companies), served as a Confederate spy, and met many important people of the era. Velazquez's extraordinary story is difficult to substantiate because most of it comes from her postwar memoir, an exaggerated, yet not wholly false, account of her wartime adventures.

Harriet Tubman did not have to hide her gender to accomplish her goals. Since African American women were rarely held to the same standards of femininity as white women, she did not need to disguise herself as a male to lead a military operation. Tubman had escaped from slavery in Maryland in 1849 but returned to the South to spirit away other fugitives. Thus, she had previous experience with covert operations when she went to South Carolina in 1862 as a nurse and scout for the Union army. Armed with a military pass, Tubman made contacts among local blacks, who provided her with information about Confederate movements. In June 1863, she led a successful military raid of black soldiers along the Combahee River, which liberated 750 slaves and destroyed several plantations belonging to prominent slave-owning families. Northern newspapers credited Tubman's forces with having "dashed into the enemy's country, striking terror into the heart of rebeldom."

"Daughters of the Regiment" were not required to hide their gender when joining a military unit. Many Daughters served only in an honorary capacity, but others actually accompanied their units into the field. Daughters on the front lines were usually the wives of soldiers in the same regiment; they saw the role of Daughter as an opportunity to serve in the war and remain close to their husbands. Annie Etheridge initially followed her husband into the Michigan infantry, but she decided to stay with the army even after he deserted. Etheridge acted as a nurse and color bearer, providing inspiration to her fellow soldiers by standing fast under fire during some of the most brutal battles of the war, including Antietam and Gettysburg. So remarkable was Etheridge's devotion that she was awarded the Kearny Cross for bravery in May 1863. Rhode Islander Kady Brownell came under fire in combat while serving in her husband's regiment as the

■ *Annie Etheridge*

Annie Etheridge's combat experience was that of a Union medic, rushing out on the field to pull wounded men from harm's way, while still in the line of fire herself.

FROM FRANK MOORE, *WOMEN OF THE WAR*, 1866

■ *Kady Brownell in uniform*

A Union "Daughter of the Regiment," Kady Brownell took her combat duties seriously by becoming a skilled swordswoman and "one of the quickest and most accurate marksmen in the regiment."

FROM FRANK MOORE,
WOMEN OF THE WAR, 1866.
LC-USZ62-110631

color bearer, and on at least one occasion saved her unit from friendly fire by rushing to the front of the line to display the identifying regimental flag. Daughters further earned the respect of their soldiers when they willingly suffered the same privations as the men, never

■ *Fanny Ricketts*

Fanny Ricketts devoted her nursing skills to her husband, who had a talent for being injured in battle. Captain James Ricketts was seriously wounded and taken prisoner in 1861, and his wife valiantly accompanied him to prison in Richmond to ensure that he received proper care. Ricketts recovered, was released from prison, and returned to active duty, only to be wounded later at the battles of Antietam and Cedar Run. Each time, Mrs. Ricketts again came to her husband's rescue and nursed him back to health.

FROM FRANK MOORE, *WOMEN OF THE WAR*, 1866

asking for special privileges. After Lucy Ann Cox died in 1891, Confederate veterans erected a monument to her service with the 30th Virginia Infantry, celebrating her as "a sharer of the toils, dangers & privations."

■ *Camp of the 31st Pennsylvania Infantry, near Washington, DC*

Some women accompanied their husbands to the war as domestics, performing useful services as cooks and laundresses for the men. This allowed families to stay together, but it also exposed women to the hardships of camp life, threats of enemy raids, and the ire of officers who disapproved of having women in camp. LC-USZC4-7983

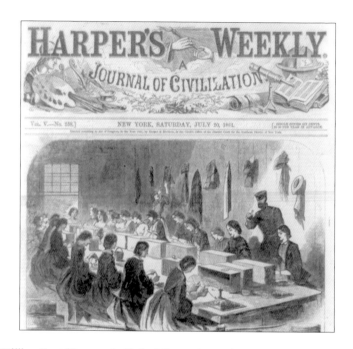

■ *"Filling Cartridges at the United States Arsenal at Watertown, Massachusetts"*

Despite this serene scene, women's work in munitions factories was very dangerous, as evidenced by fatal explosions that occurred at arsenals in Richmond and Washington. The women's voluminous dresses often helped spread fires, making it harder for female workers to escape unharmed. HARPER'S WEEKLY, JULY 20, 1861. LC-USZ62-96445

■ Woman in army garb

Women in the army modified their apparel for practical purposes, combining elements of female attire with useful military accessories. CHICAGO HISTORICAL SOCIETY

BONNET BRIGADES

Women on the Northern home front frequently turned to relief work to contribute to the war effort. The three ladies seen here, truly representatives of the "bonnet brigades," are dressed in bakers' costumes as part of a fund-raising effort. Thousands of women ventured outside their homes to put on bazaars to raise money for soldiers' relief, joined state and national aid societies, and rolled bandages for the cause— anything to show their patriotism while making life a little easier for the soldiers on the front lines.

Fairs proved to be one of the most popular and lucrative ways for women to donate their labor. Organized by Mary Livermore and Jane Hoge, the Northwestern Sanitary Fair held in Chicago in 1863 took in almost $100,000, which included $3,000 garnered by the sale of President Lincoln's manuscript version of the Emancipation Proclamation. The wild success of the Chicago fair inspired many other cities to stage similar events, and local women took active roles in organizing fairs in Boston and New York.

■ *Sanitary Commission workers*
COLLECTION OF THE NEW-YORK HISTORICAL SOCIETY

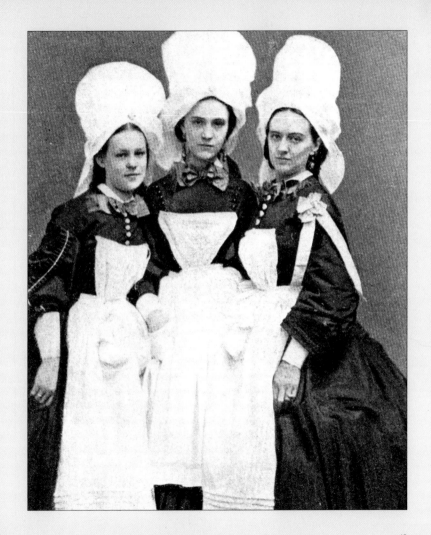

■ *Pauline Cushman in military dress*

Pauline Cushman received an honorary military commission for her spying activities for the Union. When she resurrected her acting career to recount her wartime exploits, she would sometimes dress as "Major Cushman." COLLECTION OF THE NEW-YORK HISTORICAL SOCIETY

"FEMININE DESPERADOES":
SPYING FOR THE BLUE AND GRAY

AMONG THE MORE colorful women of the Civil War were the spies, declaimed by *Frank Leslie's Illustrated Newspaper* as "feminine desperadoes." Pauline Cushman began the war as an actress, which proved good training for her role as a double agent for the Union. After clearing her plan with local authorities, Cushman pretended to be a Confederate sympathizer, resulting in her "banishment" to Tennessee. From there she traveled throughout the Confederacy, collecting information on Confederate strength in the South and the names of Confederate sympathizers operating in the North. Apparently Cushman's acting skills were not good enough to maintain her cover indefinitely, for she was arrested as a spy by Confederate General John Hunt Morgan in 1863 and sentenced to death by hanging. Cushman was saved by the opportune arrival of Union troops, but the close call could not save her spying career; by then she was too recognizable to work anonymously.

While Cushman gained wartime fame for her espionage, Elizabeth Van Lew of Richmond, Virginia, suffered hardship for her exploits. Something of an abolitionist, Van Lew remained loyal to the Union during the war and led a Richmond spy ring, communicating through the use of cipher codes, invisible ink, and messages smuggled in her servants' hollow shoe heels. She also aroused suspicion by

■ *Pauline Cushman* LC-DIG-CWPBH-02835

visiting Union prisoners confined in Richmond prisons. All these activities inspired only contempt for Van Lew among most Richmonders, who considered her a traitor to the Confederacy. "I do not know how they can call me a spy," she responded, "serving my own country within its recognized borders." Either way, Van Lew's devotion to the Union cost her most of her fortune and her standing in the community.

■ *Belle Boyd*

In addition to penning her memoir, Belle Boyd in Camp and Prison, *Boyd took to the stage after the war to recount her exciting wartime adventures.*

LC-DIG-CWPBH-01987

Other Southern women passionately supported the Confederacy and devoted their energies to undermining the Union. Belle Boyd was perhaps the most famous rebel spy, purportedly getting her start as a partisan by shooting a Union soldier who insulted her mother as he raised a United States flag over the Boyd home. Boyd soon began charming the enemy instead, using her feminine attractions to get military information she could pass along to the Confederates. Indeed, General Thomas "Stonewall" Jackson credited Boyd with providing intelligence crucial to his successful campaign in the Shenandoah Valley in 1862. As daring and successful as Boyd's spying missions were, she could not always escape detection by Union authorities and was imprisoned several times during the war, earning at least one stay at Old Capitol Prison in Washington, DC, where her defiant behavior won her the admiration of fellow captives. Ironically, this belle of the Confederacy married a Yankee sailor in 1864.

Another inmate at Old Capitol Prison was Rose O'Neal Greenhow, a member of Washington, DC's social elite, but also a Confederate spy. She began her espionage activities early in the war, when she still counted important politicians among her friends. Greenhow transmitted coded messages to a Confederate operative, who used her information to warn General P. G. T. Beauregard that Union troops were moving toward Manassas, Virginia, in 1861. The Union defeat at Manassas, and Greenhow's openly Southern sympathies, prompted Union detective Allan Pinkerton to put her under house arrest at "Fort

■ *Rose Greenhow and daughter at Old Capitol Prison, Washington, DC*

When Rose Greenhow was sent to Old Capitol Prison for spying for the Confederacy, her equally defiant eight-year-old daughter, "Little Rose," went with her. Interestingly, when Greenhow first came to Washington as a girl, she lived at the old Capitol building when her aunt ran it as a boardinghouse. LC-DIG-CWPBH-04849

Greenhow," which became an unofficial prison for women suspected of treason in Washington. Greenhow still managed to communicate with the rebels, which landed her at Old Capitol Prison for five months in 1862, after which she was exiled to the Confederacy. She then traveled through Europe, writing her memoirs. When homesickness got the better of her, she tried to return to the South in 1864. Unfortunately, her ship was overtaken by Union gunboats, and Greenhow decided to make a break for the shore rather than be captured again. Her lifeboat capsized, and Greenhow drowned, some say because she was loaded down with gold she had brought home for the Confederate cause.

"HOW TO DEAL WITH FEMALE TRAITORS"

Among the punishments for "female traitors" comically suggested by this *Harper's Weekly* cartoon is forcing them to wear straight skirts. Such a penalty not only would have made them unfashionable, but also would have hindered women from smuggling contraband under their wide hoop skirts. Southern women became particularly skilled at this; until Union officials caught on, they were not likely to offend a woman by searching her.

Women proved quite adept pack mules: "We made a balmoral of the Gray cloth for the uniforms," one woman recalled, "pin'd the Hats to the inside of my hoops, tied the boots with a strong list, letting them fall directly in front. . . . All my buttons, brass buttons, Money &c in my bosom."

656

Make them wear uniform as. e.g. the above

MRS. ——

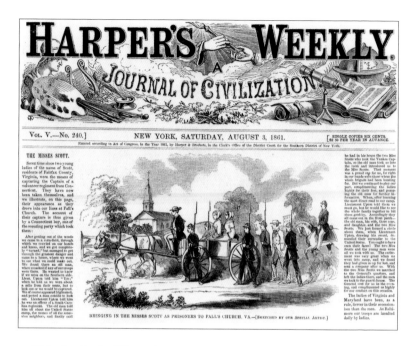

HARPER'S WEEKLY.

JOURNAL OF CIVILIZATION.

VOL. V.—No. 240.] NEW YORK, SATURDAY, AUGUST 3, 1861. [SINGLE COPIES SIX CENTS.
$2.50 PER YEAR IN ADVANCE.

Entered according to Act of Congress, in the Year 1861, by Harper & Brothers, in the Clerk's Office of the District Court for the Southern District of New York.

BRINGING IN THE MISSES SCOTT AS PRISONERS TO FALL'S CHURCH, VA.—[SKETCHED BY OUR SPECIAL ARTIST.]

■ *"Bringing In the Misses Scott"*

Although suspected of being "rank secessionists," the Misses Scott of Falls Church, Virginia, managed to charm Captain Kellogg of the 2nd Connecticut Infantry into escorting them home, where he was captured by rebel pickets. The ladies themselves were arrested through similar subterfuge by Union troops. The sisters proclaimed their innocence and were released, but not before their story had been splashed across the front page of Harper's Weekly. HARPER'S WEEKLY, AUGUST 3, 1861. COURTESY OF THE MARY RILEY STYLES PUBLIC LIBRARY, FALLS CHURCH, VIRGINIA

GENERAL STUART'S NEW AID.

■ *"General Stuart's New Aid"*

Many Southern women were accomplished riders and put their skills to the test as couriers for the Confederacy. Belle Boyd purportedly completed a hard ride to give Stonewall Jackson timely intelligence about Union troops in the Shenandoah Valley, yielding to "neither weeds nor fences" in her path. HARPER'S WEEKLY, APRIL 4, 1863. LC-USZ62-100253

■ *Antonia Ford*

Antonia Ford charmed Union General Edwin Stoughton and then alerted the Confederates to his plans and whereabouts, leading to his capture by Confederate Colonel John S. Mosby in 1863. Stoughton had spent so much time in Ford's company that one of his soldiers predicted that "if Stoughton gets picked up some night, he may thank her for it." Union authorities thus immediately suspected Ford's complicity in the general's capture, and she foolishly offered damning evidence to an undercover agent sent to investigate her. Ford subsequently spent several months in Old Capitol Prison. WILLARD FAMILY PAPERS. LCMS-45757-3

■ *Major Joseph Willard*

One of Antonia Ford's guards, Major Joseph Willard (co-owner of the famous Willard Hotel in Washington, DC), fell in love with her. She refused his advances as long as he remained a Union officer, so he resigned from the army to marry Ford in 1864. "I knew I could not revenge myself on the nation," Ford jokingly wrote of her marriage, "but was fully capable of tormenting one Yankee to death, so took the Major." Alas, the Willards' happy marriage was cut short by Antonia's death in 1871.

WILLARD FAMILY PAPERS. LC-MS-45757-2

■ *Poem, lace cap, and collar*
made by Antonia Ford at Old Capitol Prison

To pass the time while incarcerated in Old Capitol Prison, Antonia Ford made
a lace cap and collar, which she sent to her mother, along with a
patriotic poem—patriotic to the Confederacy, of course.

WILLARD FAMILY PAPERS, MANUSCRIPT DIVISION. LC-MSS-45757-7

This collar my Mamma must wear,
And she must wear alone;
I've made it in my prison cell—
Dont think me quite a drone.

And as I wrought it I have thought
Of her, my Parent dear,
And said with every stitch I made,
I would that she were here.

Not here confined by iron bars,
And locked in with a key;
But only as a visitor,
To spend the day with me.

I've watched and waited long for her
And looked out every day;
But now I murmur, will she come
Before the eighth of May.

For that day I shall be removed.

■ *A ward in Armory Square Hospital, Washington, DC*

The most modern of all Washington's Civil War hospitals, Armory Square was a plum assignment for nurses, like those seen here. But female nurses served in most Washington hospitals, including the smaller Union Hotel Hospital, in which author Louisa May Alcott took a turn. Alcott soon contracted a severe case of typhoid, which cut short her nursing career and forced her return home to Concord, Massachusetts. However, she fictionalized her brief nursing experiences in Hospital Sketches *(1863), and she infused Civil War themes into her later writings, including her famous novel* Little Women *(1868).*

LC-USZC4-7976

ANGELS OF THE BATTLEFIELDS:
FEMALE MEDICAL PERSONNEL

TODAY, NURSING IS a profession dominated by women, but it was quite the reverse during the Civil War. Nurses were typically disabled soldiers, as women were thought to be too delicate for the rigors of nursing and too respectable for exposure to male bodies. Thus, the thousands of women who ultimately left home to become nurses often had to prove themselves up to the job, especially to skeptical medical professionals in the military. Nurses had to be prepared to take on a variety of roles. They might be called on to assist in surgery (especially amputations), clean wounds, cook, do laundry, clean hospital wards, dispense medications, read and write letters for soldiers, and generally comfort the men under their charge.

Clara Barton did not go through official channels to be a nurse; she simply became one on her own. Barton solicited donations of food and medical supplies from Northern friends, which she and her assistants transported to hospitals at or near the front lines. She was shocked by the appalling conditions of the hospitals, but would not be deterred from doing whatever needed to be done, whether it be cleaning floors, administering food and comfort to patients, or bandaging their wounds. Barton's timing was impeccable. She usually arrived when the surgeons were the most overwhelmed and low on supplies. "If heaven ever sent out a homely angel," one surgeon commented, "she must be

■ *Clara Barton*

This "Angel of the Battlefield" had to fight her own demons during the war to overcome her small physical stature (she stood only five feet tall), intense shyness, crippling bouts of depression, and fears that relief work would compromise her femininity. LC-USZ62-19319

> MEMORANDA.
>
> Samuel Willis. Co S.
> 1st N.E. cavalry.— R.S.
>
> Jimri T. Allen of New Bedford,
> member of Co. C. U.S. Engineers, died
> at the Arsenal, Washington D.C. Jan.
> 9, 1862. Buried in the Congressional
> Burying Ground or Burial site
> No 81 — Range 71 —
>
> Sereno Newton . 25th Regt. Co. K.
> William Uiswell   25 " "   Co. G.
> Alfred Kisly   25 " "   " K
> William Bond   25 " .   " K.
> John Moulten   25   K.
> Otis Cooper   2.5 .   K.

■ *Page from Clara Barton's diary, December 1862*

While nursing soldiers after the battle of Fredericksburg, Barton used her pocket diary to keep notes about the men who were wounded, those who died, and where they were buried. At the end of the war, she established a bureau to help families locate missing soldiers. CLARA BARTON PAPERS. MANUSCRIPT DIVISION

MOTHER BICKERDYKE

Most women who became wartime nurses brought with them only the medical skills they had honed while taking care of their own families. Mary Ann Bickerdyke, however, had been a nurse before the war, and she built on that experience to become one of the most respected authorities on sanitary conditions in Union camps and hospitals. When her patients needed healthy food, clean clothes, or even kindling to keep them warm on the battlefield, she provided supplies by any means necessary, even if it involved shipping a thousand chickens down the Mississippi River. Bickerdyke's reputation gave her an air of authority that even generals hesitated to challenge. When she had a drunken assistant surgeon discharged from the army, he complained to General William T. Sherman. "Who caused the discharge?" Sherman asked. Told that Bickerdyke was responsible, Sherman replied, "If that is the case, I can do nothing for you. She ranks me." With that sort of influence, travel passes (such as the one seen here) may have been only a formality. Ironically, the woman whom soldiers affectionately nicknamed "Mother Bickerdyke" had left her own young sons with friends in order to join the war effort.

■ **Mary Ann Bickerdyke**

FROM FRANK MOORE,
WOMEN OF THE WAR, 1866

■ *Military pass, 1863*

MARY ANN BALL BICKERDYKE PAPERS. MANUSCRIPT DIVISION

■ *Susie King Taylor*

Only a teenager when she escaped slavery, Susie King Taylor became a laundress for a Union regiment of African American soldiers. Her duties eventually expanded to include cooking, nursing, and teaching (she had secretly learned to read as a child). She later wrote a memoir of her time in the military, one of the few to have been written by an African American woman who served during the war.

FROM HER *REMINISCENCES OF MY LIFE IN CAMP*, 1902.
LC-USZ61-1863

one, her assistance was so timely." Barton literally risked her life for her relief work. At the battle of Antietam, a soldier taking a sip of water from Barton's cup was shot by a stray bullet and died in her arms, the bullet having first passed through the sleeve of Barton's dress. Her steadiness under fire proved her mettle, yet she could also comfort the wounded with a womanly touch, both of which earned the respect of the soldiers she served. This relief work became the defining experience of Barton's life and later inspired her to organize the American Red Cross in 1881.

Confederate women were no less dedicated to their nursing duties than were Union women. Kate Cumming left her home in Alabama to help nurse soldiers after the battle of Shiloh; she was kept so busy her first week that ten days passed before she could change her blood-stained dress. Still, she remained with the Confederate Army of Tennessee until 1865. Juliet Opie Hopkins also left Alabama for Richmond, where she became the superintendent of Alabama's hospitals, charged with hiring staff and overseeing hospital administration, until she broke her leg while supervising the removal of wounded soldiers from a battlefield in 1863. Phoebe Pember served the Confederacy through her work as head matron of a ward of Richmond's massive Chimborazo Hospital. Despite her track record—by the end of the war, she had attended to over fifteen thousand soldiers—her toughest battles were with the male hospital staff, who resented the presence of a woman, and with the female contract laborers, whom she considered her social inferiors.

If female nurses had to be daring to succeed, the few women doctors who participated in the war effort had to be doubly so. Having received a medical degree in 1855, Dr. Mary E. Walker immediately offered to serve in the US Army's medical corps after the war began. The military refused to commission her as a doctor, and she refused to accept a lesser appointment as a nurse, so Walker went to war as a

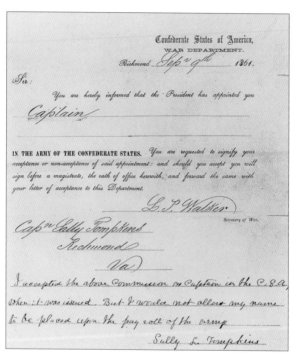

Confederate States of America,
WAR DEPARTMENT.

Richmond *Sep 9th* 1861.

Sir:

You are hereby informed that the President has appointed you

Captain

IN THE ARMY OF THE CONFEDERATE STATES. You are requested to signify your acceptance or non-acceptance of said appointment: and should you accept you will sign before a magistrate, the oath of office herewith, and forward the same with your letter of acceptance to this Department.

L. P. Walker
Secretary of War.

Capn Sally Tompkins
Richmond
Va

I accepted the above Commission as Captain in the C.S.A. when it was issued. But I would not allow my name to be placed upon the pay roll of the army

Sally L. Tompkins

■ **Sally Tompkins' commission, 1861**

When the Confederate government closed many of Richmond's private hospitals in 1861 to centralize medical care, Robertson Hospital was spared by granting Sally Tompkins a military commission. Funding the hospital herself, Tompkins kept it operating until the end of the war, with admirably low mortality rates.

THE MUSEUM OF THE CONFEDERACY, RICHMOND, VIRGINIA. PHOTOGRAPH BY KATHERINE WETZEL

volunteer physician, receiving only rations and shelter in return. After serving in a hospital ward in Washington, she left for the front, where she tended to wounded soldiers after the battle of Fredericksburg in 1862. For the first two years of the war, she traveled with the army, earning the respect of both the soldiers and medical professionals with whom she served. "She can amputate a limb with the skill of an old surgeon," a newspaper reported, although Walker would privately advise soldiers to refuse amputations urged by other doctors when she thought the limb might be saved. In 1864, she scored a partial victory with an appointment as a noncommissioned contract surgeon for the 52nd Ohio Infantry—not a regular commission, but at least a recognized medical position. In addition to tending to her own soldiers, Walker ventured into the Tennessee countryside to minister to the civilian population, an act of altruism that resulted in her capture by Confederates and subsequent imprisonment at Castle Thunder in Richmond in 1864. After being exchanged for an imprisoned Confederate officer, she became the surgeon in charge at the female military prison in Louisville, Kentucky. There, Walker faced hostility from both the female Confederate inmates and her male supervisors, leading her to request a transfer just before the war ended.

Despite the hardships female medical personnel may have initially encountered, and the difficult and gory circumstances under which they labored, many nurses relished the experience of ministering to wounded soldiers. *"It is life,"* one nurse confessed, "and we wouldn't be anywhere else for anything in the world."

■ *Dr. Mary Edwards Walker*

*As a doctor, Mary Walker found long skirts
unsanitary in that they picked up blood and
dirt as hems dragged along the floor.
Instead, she routinely wore pants under a
short skirt, which allowed her freedom of
movement. After the war, she gave up skirts
entirely, adopting men's fashions
and short hairstyles.*

LC-USZ62-112180

*Most postwar photographs of
Dr. Walker also show her wearing
her Congressional Medal of Honor, which
President Andrew Johnson bestowed upon
her in recognition of her medical contribu-
tions to the war effort. In 1917, Walker
was one of nine hundred recipients stripped
of their awards on a technicality, but she
refused to surrender her medal and
proudly wore it until her death in 1919.
The award was restored in 1977.*

LC-USZ62-62752

■ *Michigan Soldiers' Relief Association in Virginia, 1864*

After discovering that her wounded brother had died before she arrived in Virginia, Julia Wheelock (far left) decided to stay and join the Michigan Soldiers' Relief Association, where she could "do for others as I would have done for my brother." Wheelock visited hospitals and battlefields in Virginia, distributing supplies and lending a sympathetic ear to soldiers from her home state. Independent state relief agencies afforded other women the chance to serve, as was the case for Annie Wittenmyer, the guiding force of the Keokuk (Iowa) Ladies' Soldiers' Aid Society. Wittenmyer pioneered the concept of "special diet kitchens" to provide wounded soldiers with food appropriate to their medical conditions.

■ *Nurses and officers of the United States Sanitary Commission at Fredericksburg, Virginia, 1864*

The civilian United States Sanitary Commission distributed food, provided medical facilities, and offered other goods and services not adequately supplied by the government. Women served throughout the ranks of the USSC as nurses, fund-raisers, and agents, although the highest administrative positions were reserved for men. LC-DIG-CWPB-01195

THE RELATION

OF

THE NATIONAL GOVERNMENT

TO

THE REVOLTED CITIZENS

DEFINED.

NO POWER IN CONGRESS TO EMANCIPATE THEIR SLAVES OR CONFISCATE
THEIR PROPERTY PROVED.

THE CONSTITUTION AS IT IS, THE ONLY HOPE OF THE COUNTRY.

By ANNA ELLA CARROLL.

Congress has now under consideration, the question of the power and expediency of abolishing slavery, and confiscating the property, real and personal, of all, or a large class of the rebels in arms. A question of more transcendent importance, than any that ever before, engaged the attention of the American people.

With an earnest desire that the country may not be led to the adoption of a mistaken and fatal policy, I propose now to contribute my best efforts to a further understanding of this vital subject.

No one doubts the power or the duty of the Government to suppress the rebellion, to use the army and navy, and all the military resources of the country to capture the rebels, and kill them if they will not submit, and destroy their power to war upon us. But, I do not think there is any grant in the Constitution, but rather an express inhibition upon the power of Congress to abolish slavery or confiscate the property of rebels.

There are two clauses in the Constitution which especially refer to the confiscation of property. The first defines the crime of treason, and authorizes Congress to prescribe the punishment; inhibiting, however, the confiscation of property beyond the life of the offender. The second is an absolute prohibition to Congress of confiscation altogether. The first defines the crime in these words: "Treason against the United States shall consist in levying war against them, or in adhering to their enemies, giving them aid and comfort. No person shall be convicted of treason unless on the testimony of two witnesses to the same overt act, or on confession in open court." "The Congress shall have power to declare the punishment of treason, but no attainder of treason shall work corruption of blood, or forfeiture, except during the life of the person attained."

Treason is not an offense against society, but an offense against its government; and in all ages, a disposition has been evinced on the part of the governing power, to construe everything as treason which opposed it. And this arises from the natural passion of revenge, the desire to punish for opposition to its authority, the rapac-

"THE EFFECT OF HER GENIUS":
PROPAGANDISTS FOR THE CAUSE

SOME CIVIL WAR–ERA women demonstrated their daring by using their voices or the power of their pens to further political causes. Anna Ella Carroll of Maryland had been a pamphleteer prior to the war, so it was a natural transition for her to write for the US government during the war. Her 1861 *Reply to Breckinridge,* justifying President Lincoln's policies during the secession crisis, brought her to the attention of the War Department and led to an unofficial agreement for her to produce propaganda pieces. Unfortunately, the agreement did not specify her compensation, and when Carroll later submitted a claim for $50,000 for her labors, Lincoln himself declared it "the most outrageous one ever made to any government on earth." In a bit of self-promotion, Carroll also tried to take credit for suggesting the military campaigns on the Tennessee and Cumberland Rivers that led to Union victories at Forts Henry and Donelson. While Carroll may have passed along valuable information she gathered from an experienced

■ *Pamphlet, c. 1862, by Anna Ella Carroll*

Anna Ella Carroll disagreed with the government's policy of confiscating slaves during the war, and her dissent took the form of the pamphlet on the preceding page.

AFRICAN AMERICAN PAMPHLET COLLECTION, AMERICAN MEMORY WEBSITE

■ *Schoolteachers at Norfolk, 1865*

The freeing of millions of slaves from bondage created a desperate need in the Union-occupied South for missionaries and teachers to help with the transition from slavery to freedom. The Chase sisters of Massachusetts, among the group above, were so moved by the challenges faced by former slaves that they left their comfortable home and secured positions as teachers in order to work among the freedmen and freedwomen in Virginia.

THE WESTERN RESERVE HISTORICAL SOCIETY, CLEVELAND, OHIO

■ *Gideonites in South Carolina*

The conditions under which Northern teachers, such as the Gideonite missionaries seen above, labored could be potentially dangerous. Charlotte Forten taught in South Carolina and so feared raids by Confederates who had sworn violence against teachers that she armed herself as a precaution. Substandard housing and the fleas Forten described as "horrible little tyrants" added to the challenges teachers and missionaries had to endure.

THE WESTERN RESERVE HISTORICAL SOCIETY, CLEVELAND, OHIO

riverboat captain, her ideas had been duplicated elsewhere, making her claim as a strategist dubious at best.

Anna Dickinson used oratory to further the war effort, stumping for the Republican Party as well as for abolitionism and women's rights. Although only in her twenties, she was so famous that she commanded a $1,000 speaking fee in 1863, at a time when ordinary soldiers received just $13 per month. Dickinson's youthful appearance belied the reach of her fame as an orator during the Civil War. Frederick Douglass called her "a lady of marvelous eloquence"; others noted that her vivid oratory "brought down the house with thunders of applause."

Dickinson reached the pinnacle of her wartime career in January 1864, when she was invited by members of Congress to address the House of Representatives. There, Vice President Hamlin gave an introductory speech in which he compared her to Joan of Arc. By then, Dickinson's fierce rhetoric included denunciation of Lincoln's reconstruction policies, but she nonetheless thought it prudent to urge his renomination, since the president himself was in attendance. Dickinson felt no similar urge to speak kindly about the Confederates, noting in her speech that "there is not an arm of compromise in all the North long enough to stretch over the sea of blood and the mound of fallen Northern soldiers to shake hands with their murderers on the other side."

■ *Anna Dickinson*

BATTLE HYMN OF THE REPUBLIC.

BY MRS. JULIA WARD HOWE.

Mine eyes have seen the glory of the coming of the Lord:
He is trampling out the vintage where the grapes of wrath
are stored;
He hath loosed the fateful lightnings of His terrible swift sword:
His truth is marching on.
CHORUS—Glory, glory, hallelujah!
Glory, glory, hallelujah!
Glory, glory, hallelujah!
His truth is marching on.

I have seen Him in the watch-fires of a hundred circling camps;
They have builded Him an altar in the evening dews and
damps:
I can read His righteous sentence by the dim and flaring lamps:
His day is marching on.
CHORUS—Glory, glory, hallelujah, &c.
His day is marching on.

I have read a fiery gospel writ in burnished rows of steel:
"As ye deal with my contemners, so with you my grace shall
deal;
Let the Hero, born of woman, crush the serpent with his heel,
Since God is marching on."
CHORUS—Glory, glory, hallelujah &c.
Since God is marching on.

He has sounded forth the trumpet that shall never call retreat:
He is sifting out the hearts of men before His judgment seat:
Oh, be swift, my soul, to answer Him! be jubilant my feet!
Our God is marching on!
CHORUS—Glory, glory, hallelujah, &c.
Our God is marching on!

In the beauty of the lilies Christ was born across the sea,
With a glory in His bosom that transfigures you and me;
As he died to make men holy, let us die to make men free,
While God is marching on.
CHORUS—Glory, glory, hallelujah, &c.
While God is marching on.

Published by the Supervisory Committee for Recruiting Colored Regiments

■ *"Battle Hymn of the Republic," by Julia Ward Howe*

Inspired by a review of troops outside Washington, Julia Ward Howe awoke early the next morning with verses "arranging themselves in my brain." These lines became "The Battle Hymn of the Republic," one of the best known anthems of the Civil War. Writing the "Battle Hymn of the Republic" was one of the few ways Howe was able to contribute to the war effort, as her husband, Samuel G. Howe, a founder of the United States Sanitary Commission, forbade her from becoming a nurse or joining a reform movement. LIBRARY OF CONGRESS

The Confederacy boasted fewer outspoken female propagandists during the war, although several women achieved minor fame for their pro-Southern writings. In *Macaria; or, Altars of Sacrifice* (1864), novelist Augusta Jane Evans' characters defend the Confederate cause and slavery so convincingly that the novel was banned from Union camps. Southern women more frequently wielded their pens in private

Head-Quarters, Department of the Gulf,
New Orleans, May 15, 1862.

General Orders, No. 28.

As the Officers and Soldiers of the United States have been subject to repeated insults from the women calling themselves ladies of New Orleans, in return for the most scrupulous non-interference and courtesy on our part, it is ordered that hereafter when any Female shall, by word, gesture, or movement, insult or show contempt for any officer or soldier of the United States, she shall be regarded and held liable to be treated as a woman of the town plying her avocation.

By command of Maj.-Gen. **BUTLER**,
GEORGE C. STRONG,
A. A. G. Chief of Staff.

■ *Broadside*

To express their Confederate sympathies, women in Union-occupied New Orleans spit on Union troops, hurled verbal epithets at them, and even dumped the contents of chamber pots from their windows onto unsuspecting Yankees below. General Benjamin F. Butler decided to teach the rebellious women a lesson and issued his infamous "Woman Order," which declared that if the ladies did not behave themselves, they would be shown the same respect as prostitutes. The tactic worked but earned the general the nickname "Beast Butler" in the process. TULANE UNIVERSITY

"SHOOT, IF YOU MUST, THIS OLD GRAY HEAD, BUT SPARE YOUR COUNTRY'S FLAG! SHE SAID"

Barbara Frietchie

■ *Barbara Frietchie*

Poet John Greenleaf Whittier immortalized the patriotism of the elderly Barbara Frietchie, who supposedly refused to stop waving an American flag when Stonewall Jackson's troops came through Frederick, Maryland, in 1862. Contemporary observers and modern historians later debated whether it was Frietchie or a neighbor who daringly waved the flag during the event Whittier described in his poem. Frietchie herself could not testify to the poem's accuracy, as she died just weeks after the encounter with Jackson's troops.

FROM L. P. BROCKETT, *WOMAN'S WORK IN THE CIVIL WAR: A RECORD OF HEROISM, PATRIOTISM AND PATIENCE*, 1867

REAPING.

SOUTHERN WOMEN FEELING THE EFFECTS OF REBELLION, AND CREATING BREAD RIOTS.

■ *Richmond Bread Riot, 1863*

By April 1863, rampant inflation and scarcities of basic goods drove women in Richmond to loot stores in an infamous "bread riot." Were they otherwise-peaceful women compelled to steal out of desperation? An organized and effective group of protesters? Or a pack of wild rabble-rousers bent on pillaging? FROM *FRANK LESLIE'S ILLUSTRATED NEWSPAPER*, MAY 23, 1863. THE MUSEUM OF THE CONFEDERACY, RICHMOND, VIRGINIA. PHOTOGRAPH BY KATHERINE WETZEL

diaries, in which they recorded events of the war, their relative faith in Confederate leaders and the cause itself, and, often, their opinions about slavery. Although keeping a diary was not a daring act in itself, subsequent generations owe a debt to women such as Mary Chesnut and Sarah Morgan for recording such candid assessments of life in the Confederacy.

THESE WOMEN represent only a sampling of the best-known daring women of the Civil War. Others committed less colorful, but no less important, acts of daring. They sent their men off to war, ran farms and homesteads, and sometimes took jobs outside their homes for extra income or to help the cause. In doing so, these women endured their own fiery trials during the Civil War, along with the nation itself. ■

FOR FURTHER READING

Blanton, DeAnne, and Lauren M. Cook. *They Fought Like Demons: Women Soldiers in the Civil War*. Baton Rouge: Louisiana State University Press, 2002.

Clinton, Catherine, and Nina Silber, eds. *Divided Houses: Gender and the Civil War*. New York: Oxford University Press, 1992.

Hall, Richard. *Patriots in Disguise: Women Warriors of the Civil War*. New York: Paragon House, 1993.

Heidler, David S., and Jeanne T. Heidler, eds. *Encyclopedia of the American Civil War: A Political, Social, and Military History*. New York: W. W. Norton, 2000. See entries for "Women" and for individual women.

Leonard, Elizabeth D. *All the Daring of the Soldier: Women of the Civil War Armies*. New York: W. W. Norton, 1999.

———. *Yankee Women: Gender Battles in the Civil War*. New York: W. W. Norton, 1994.

Massey, Mary Elizabeth. *Women in the Civil War*. Lincoln: University of Nebraska Press, 1994. Originally published as *Bonnet Brigades*. New York: A. A. Knopf, 1966.

Moore, Frank. *Women of the War: Their Heroism and Self-Sacrifice; True Stories of Brave Women in the Civil War*. Hartford, CT: S. S. Scranton, 1866. Reprint, Alexander, NC: Blue/Gray Books, 1997.

Wagner, Margaret E., Gary W. Gallagher, and Paul Finkelman, eds. *The Library of Congress Civil War Desk Reference*. New York: Simon & Schuster, 2002.

ACKNOWLEDGMENTS

The author would like to thank Amy Pastan for overseeing this project with grace and good humor; Susan Reyburn and the Library of Congress' Publishing Office for including her as part of the team; and Pomegranate Communications for the opportunity to share these daring women's stories. Thanks also to Bradley Gernand for bringing the Misses Scott to the author's attention, and Kathleen Krowl for reading yet another manuscript.

IMAGES

Reproduction numbers, when available, are given for all items in the collections of the Library of Congress. Unless otherwise noted, Library of Congress images are from the Prints and Photographs Division. To order reproductions, note the LC- number provided with the image; where no number exists, note the Library division and the title of the item. Direct your request to:

The Library of Congress
Photoduplication Service
Washington DC 20540-4570
(202) 707-5640; www.loc.gov